THE LET'S JAM! BOOK

WITH DVD & CD

BY

PETER VOGL

JAM WITH A GREAT BAND ANYTIME YOU WANT!

The *Let's Jam! Book* with DVD & CD is a collection of lessons demonstrating specific ideas about how to jam along with a real band. The *Let's Jam! Book* includes ten tracks from the Watch & Learn *Let's Jam!* series of play along CDs. You will learn new licks and rhythms while experiencing what it is like to play with a real band. If you are taking private lessons, this material will help you to further develop and refine the skills needed to feel comfortable jamming with others. Playing with the *Let's Jam! CDs* and using the information in the *Let's Jam! Book* will have you playing with a real band in no time!

The *Let's Jam! CDs* were developed by Peter Vogl over a ten-year period of time based on his experience teaching hundreds of students. The *Let's Jam! Book* with DVD & CD provides a unique approach that gives you the materials needed to hone your playing skills and jam along with a real band. The other products in the Watch & Learn *Guitarist's Jam System* (*Let's Jam! CDs, Tablature Book, Chord Book, Scale Book, Music Theory Book, Note Reading Method, & Lick Book & DVD*) will offer you additional resources for your journey to take your playing to the next level and fit in with any real band setting!

The Guitarist's Jam System

Tab	Chord	Scale	Theory	Note Reading	Lick

The Let's Jam! CD Series

Blues & Rock	More Blues & Rock	Blues & Rock Vol 3	Country & Bluegrass	Jazz & Blues	Hard Rock	Unplugged

THE AUTHOR

Peter Vogl, the author of this book, has been a professional performer and teacher in the Atlanta area for over 20 years. He was raised in Michigan and went to college at the University of Georgia, where he majored in classical guitar performance. He also did post graduate work at James Madison University. Peter has set up and directed 6 different schools of music in the Atlanta area and currently works at Jan Smith Studios as a session player and guitar instructor. He has written several instructional courses including *Introduction to Blues Guitar, Introduction to Rock Guitar, The Guitarist's Tablature Book, The Guitarist's Chord Book, The Guitarist's Scale Book, The Guitarist's Music Theory Book, The Guitarist's Lick DVD,* and the *Let's Jam! CD Series* (seven different jam along CDs).

DVD CHAPTER MARKERS

The DVD markers are included in this book to show where each lesson is located on the companion DVD. Use your remote control on the DVD player to skip to the track you want. Also use the menu system on the DVD to locate each lick.

HOW TO USE THE BOOK, DVD, & AUDIO CD

Step 1 - Watch the DVD while following along with the book. Play along with the DVD on your guitar. Replay each chapter on the DVD until you are comfortable playing along with it.

Step 2 - When you are comfortable with a lesson or piece of music, pull out the audio CD from inside the back cover and play along with the appropriate track. Try expanding your horizons a little and stretch out your technique. Don't be afraid to experiment.

Step 3 - Go back to the book & DVD and play along to make sure you're on the right track.

TABLE OF CONTENTS

THE AUDIO CD

The audio CD inside the back cover of this book contains the ten *Let's Jam! CD* tracks that are used in this course. After going through each lesson in the book and watching it on the DVD, you should go to the CD and play along with the track. These are taken from three different Watch & Learn *Let's Jam! CD* discs. Here's a list of the tracks:

Track	Title	Let's Jam! Disc
1.	Em7 A13	Let's Jam! CD Jazz & Blues
2.	Am Blues	Let's Jam! CD Blues & Rock
3.	D Rock Groove	Let's Jam! CD More Blues & Rock
4.	Gm Blues	Let's Jam! CD More Blues & Rock
5.	Not Too Excited	Let's Jam! CD More Blues & Rock
6.	G Shuffle	Let's Jam! CD Blues & Rock
7.	Rock'n Blues In G	Let's Jam! CD Jazz & Blues
8.	Funk In E	Let's Jam! CD Blues & Rock
9.	Roadhouse In A	Let's Jam! CD Jazz & Blues
10.	E Bluesy Rock	Let's Jam! CD More Blues & Rock

SECTION 1
TUNING & TECHNIQUES

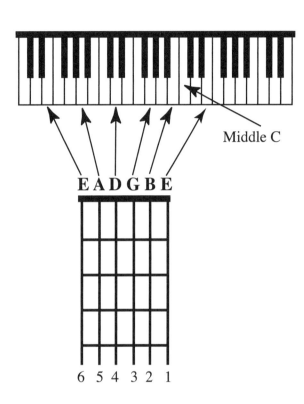

TUNING THE GUITAR

Before playing the guitar, it must be tuned to standard pitch. If you have a piano at home, it can be used as a tuning source. The following picture shows which note on the piano to tune each open string of the guitar to.

Note: If your piano hasn't been tuned recently, it is not a reliable pitch reference. Neglected pianos gradually drop in pitch over time and can be considerably flat. In this case, use one of the following methods to tune.

Middle C

E A D G B E

6 5 4 3 2 1

DVD

It is recommended that you tune your guitar to the DVD that accompanies this book so that you will be in tune when you play along with the songs and exercises.

ELECTRONIC TUNER

An electronic tuner is the fastest and most accurate way to tune a guitar. I highly recommend getting one. They are available for $20 - $50.

TIP *Purchase a music stand. People who use one tend to practice up to 30% longer.*

RELATIVE TUNING

Relative tuning means to tune the guitar to itself and is used in the following situations:

1. When you do not have an electronic tuner or other source to tune from.
2. When you have only one note to tune from.

In the following example we will tune all of the strings to the 6th string of the guitar, which is an E note.

1. Place the ring finger of the left hand behind the fifth fret of the 6th string to fret the 1st note. Tune the 5th string open (not fretted) until it sounds like the 6th string fretted at the 5th fret.
2. Fret the 5th string at the 5th fret. Tune the 4th string open (not fretted) until it sounds like the 5th string at the 5th fret.
3. Fret the 4th string at the 5th fret. Tune the 3rd string open until it sounds like the 4th string at the 5th fret.
4. Fret the 3rd string at the 4th fret. Tune the 2nd string until it sounds like the 3rd string at the 4th fret.
5. Fret the 2nd string at the 5th fret. Tune the 1st string open until it sounds like the 2nd string at the 5th fret.
Now repeat the above procedure to fine tune the guitar. Until your ear develops, have your teacher or a guitar playing friend check the tuning to make sure it is correct.

The following diagram of the guitar fret board illustrates the above procedure.

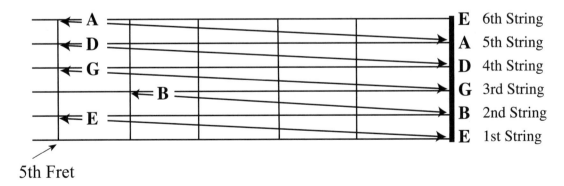

5th Fret

Note - Old dull strings lose their tonal qualities and sometimes tune incorrectly. Check with your teacher or favorite music store to make sure your strings are in good playing condition.

TABLATURE

This book is written in both tablature and standard music notation. If you wish to learn to read music, try *The Guitarist's Note Reading Book* by Watch & Learn. We will explain tablature because it is easy to learn if you are teaching yourself and because a lot of popular guitar music is available in tablature.

Tablature is a system for writing music that shows the proper string and fret to play and which fingers to use. In guitar tablature, each line represents a string on the guitar. If the string is to be fretted, the fret number is written on the appropriate line. Otherwise a 0 is written. Study the examples below until you understand them thoroughly.

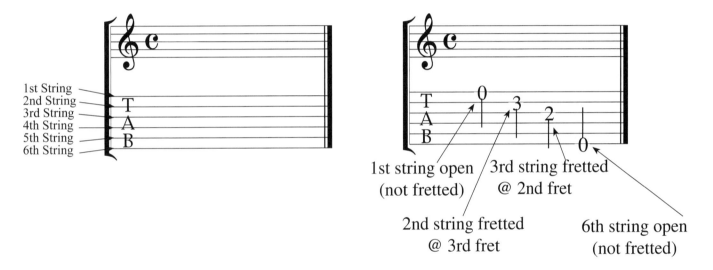

1st String
2nd String
3rd String
4th String
5th String
6th String

1st string open (not fretted)
2nd string fretted @ 3rd fret
3rd string fretted @ 2nd fret
6th string open (not fretted)

The music will be divided into either two sets of lines (staffs) or three sets of lines.

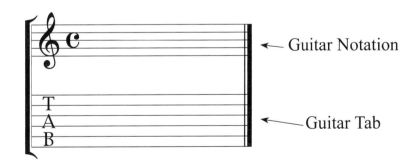

Guitar Notation

Guitar Tab

WHAT FRETS MEAN TO YOU

Frets are the little metal bars on the neck of the guitar. When pressing down on a string in a fret space, the sound of the note comes from the fret in front of the finger (or to the left in the photo below). This is very important. What this means is **when we are pressing down any string in any fret, we are not trying to hold the string against the wood of the guitar neck**. (Read above phrase again as reinforcement). We are holding the string down so it touches the fret in front of it.

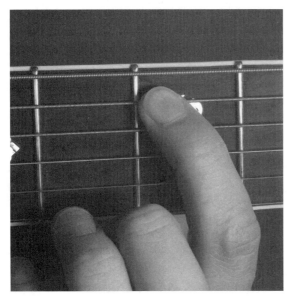 

Finger at front of fret and good position   **Finger in back of fret and poor position**

CHORD DIAGRAMS

In this book you will find chord diagrams that will help you visualize where fingers should be placed on the guitar. Study the diagram below so that you will understand these diagrams when you see them.

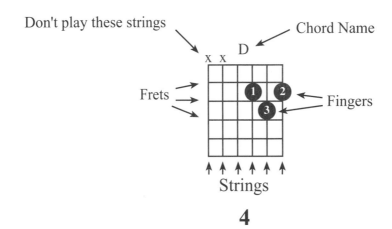

4

TECHNIQUES

Here are some fundamental techniques that are required for this book. If you are having difficulty with these techniques, try the *Intro To Rock Guitar* or *Intro To Blues Guitar* Book and DVD. They both clearly explain and demonstrate these techniques.

HAMMER ONS AND PULL OFFS

When playing a hammer on, pick the first note, then hammer on with a finger on your left hand. You will need to be on the tip of the finger and strike the note with velocity and accuracy.

When playing a pull off, again pick the first note, then pull off with a finger on your left hand. You will need to be on the tip of the finger. The finger you are pulling off to needs to hold the string stable during the pull off.

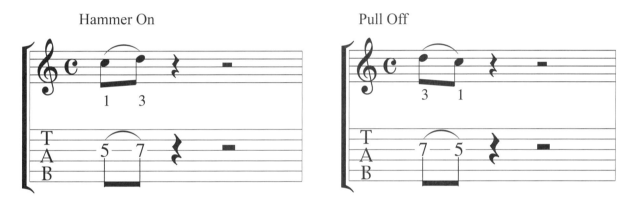

DOUBLE HAMMER ONS AND PULL OFFS

A double hammer on is executed by picking the first note and hammering on the next two notes. When pulling off, you should feel as if you're plucking the string with your finger. Both techniques require you to be on the tip of your fingers.

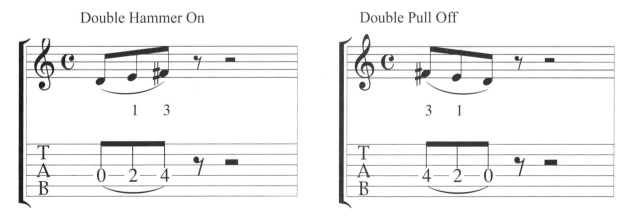

HAMMER ON PULL OFF COMBINATION

This technique starts by picking the first note, hammering on, and then pulling off back to the first note.

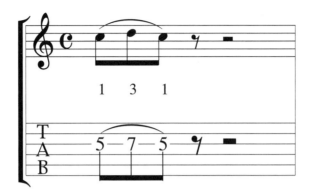

TRILLS

A trill is a repeated hammer on and pull off. Be sure to be on the tips of your fingers.

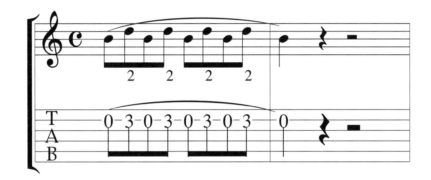

VIBRATO

A vibrato is a technique mostly used on the notes that are held or sustained for a while, like a last note of a phrase. It is a rhythmic moving of the string. Vibratos can be many speeds, from fast to slow.

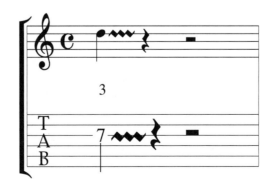

SLIDES

A slide means you pick a note and slide into another. Slides can move up or down and can be phrased many different ways.

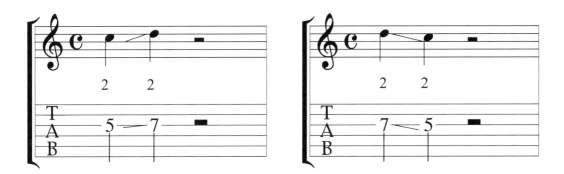

SLIDES FROM A UNDETERMINED NOTE

This slide usually starts a fret or two away but sometimes further. It does not stay at the starting point long enough for the listener to really tell where it starts.

DOUBLE STOP SLIDES

This is a slide involving two notes. It is important that both fingers move evenly across the frets.

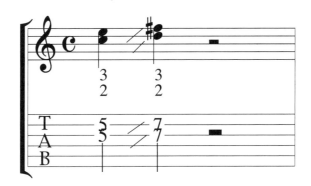

BENDS

When playing a bend, use all the fingers that are available to help execute the bend. With a third finger, for example, use the third finger to bend the note, the second finger on the same string helping to bend the note, and the first finger to mute the string above it. Compare the sound of your bends, hammer ons, and vibratos with the DVD to make sure they sound the same.

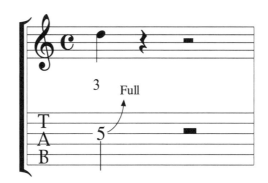

BEND WITH A STATIONARY NOTE

Use your pinky to hold the note stationary on the first string and use the third and second finger to bend the second string a whole step. You can play them both at the same time or one after the other.

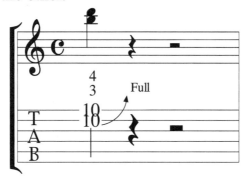

HAMMER ON BEND

This is a very legato sound. Hammer on to the 7th fret and then bend the note a whole step. You only pick the first note.

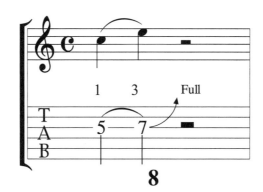

LICKS & PHRASING

After learning to play a lick as written, another valuable step is to practice phrasing the same lick many different ways. This will enable you to make the lick your own and to possibly come up with a completely new lick based on your new phrasing. Phrasing refers to the manner in which you play music. It generally refers to rhythm, tempo, accents, and dynamics. In this case, it means to change the rhythm or try a different accent pattern. Try changing the speed or feel of the lick. Try the lick against different songs or jam tracks. Go as far as changing the order of notes or repeating one or subtracting a note or two.

Here is an example lick. Listen to the DVD to hear how I phrase this lick several different ways.

Try this technique with as many licks as possible. Learn the lick, then try to change it. Make it your own idea and make it a logical, musical one. There is no right or wrong way, just choices to be made. One song or track might inspire a different phrasing than another. This does not mean you shouldn't learn the lick as written. Try learning the rule before you break it.

PLAYING WITH
Em7 A13

FROM
LET'S JAM! CD JAZZ & BLUES

Track 1 on the audio CD
included with this book.

1. Learn the E minor pentatonic scale - p11

2. Play the scale with the track at three speeds - p11

3. Learn three licks with the track - p12

A great way to use *Let's Jam! CDs* is to practice scales that are right for the track.

Exercise 1

Practice the first position E minor pentatonic scale first using quarter notes. Play along with the DVD.

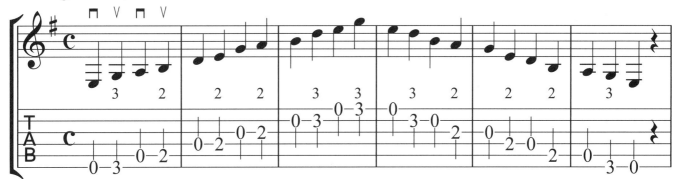

Exercise 2

Practice the first position E minor pentatonic scale using eighth notes. This will be twice as fast as exercise 1. Play along with the DVD.

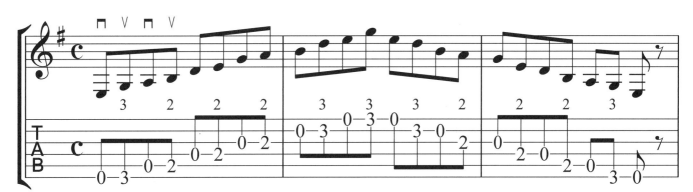

Exercise 3

Practice the first position E minor pentatonic scale using sixteenth notes. This will be twice as fast as exercise 2. Play along with the DVD.

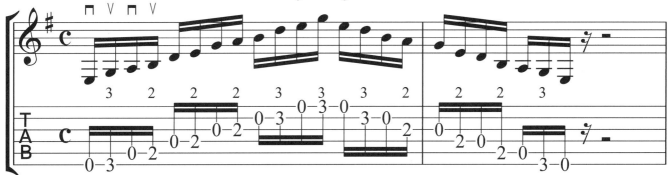

Take each exercise and play the scales repeatedly over the track. You can start on any beat, but make sure to play in time.

11

LICKS OVER Em7 A13

Perhaps the most common way to practice with *Let's Jam! CD* tracks is to practice licks and hone them so you can use them when playing with others. **Licks** are memorized combinations of notes and rhythms that players use repeatedly. Once you are proficient with licks and scales, you can combine them into entire solos. Here are three licks that are great to practice over this track.

Lick 1

This lick is out of the E minor pentatonic scale. Practice it slowly, then try it with the DVD.

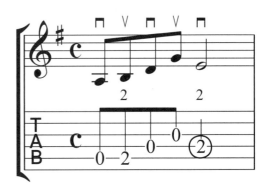

Lick 2

Lick 2 has a pull off on the 3rd string and is again out of the Em pentatonic scale. Practice it until it is smooth and then play it with the DVD.

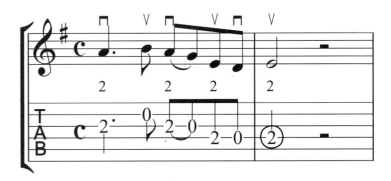

Lick 3

This lick uses the Em pentatonic scale and has a pull off on the 1st string. Notice this lick starts on the second half of beat one. Practice it on it's own and then play it over the DVD.

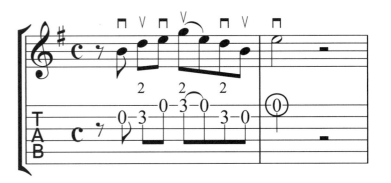

You can find many more licks and several complete solos in *The Guitarist's Lick Book*.

TIP!
Keep your guitar looking good with guitar polish. Never use furniture polish or cleaner.

PLAYING WITH
Am BLUES

FROM
LET'S JAM! CD BLUES & ROCK

Track 2 on the audio CD
included with this book.

1. Learn the A minor pentatonic scale - p14

2. Play the scale with the track at three speeds - p14

3. Learn three licks with the track - p15

4. Learn a solo to play with the track - p16

Start this section by working on the A minor pentatonic scale. Remember each track on a *Let's Jam! CD* has a scale suggestion inside the booklet. Try practicing the A minor pentatonic scales below.

19-20

Exercise 4

Practice along with the DVD playing the first position A minor pentatonic scale using quarter notes.

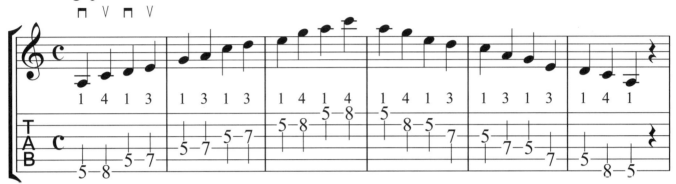

21

Exercise 5

Practice playing the first position A minor pentatonic scale using eighth notes. This will be twice as fast as Exercise 4.

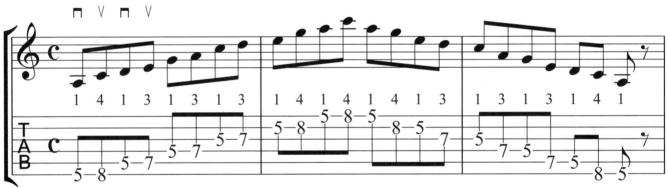

22-23

Exercise 6

Practice playing the first position A minor pentatonic scale using sixteenth notes. This will be twice as fast as Exercise 5.

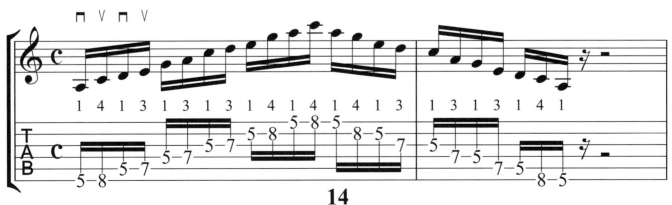

LICKS OVER Am BLUES

This track is great for minor pentatonic licks and blues licks. Most solos we hear have a heavy lick component. **Licks** are memorized combinations of notes and rhythms that players use repeatedly. Guitar players are constantly looking for more licks.

Lick 4

This lick uses passing tones which are in between notes in the scale. The main structure of this lick is the Am pentatonic scale.

Lick 5

This lick starts just after the start of beat 3. It is easier to feel this lick than count it. Practice slowly and then try it over the DVD.

Lick 6

This lick uses the blues note to start the lick. For more information on blues scales, try page 78 of the "more scales" section of *The Guitarist's Scale Book*.

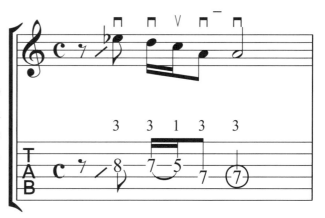

After working through this book you will find more licks and more advanced licks in *The Guitarist's Lick Book*.

TIP!

Working with a metronome helps you practice slowly and gradually increase speed.

A MINOR SOLO

In this section we have taken the three licks we just learned and combined them into a solo. Most guitar solos are combinations of licks, scales, arpeggios, and many other melodic ideas a guitarist might have. In this case, we have limited ourselves to the licks we have learned in this section with the exception of adding one note late in the solo to help it sound better. Practice it first slowly without the track and then play it up to speed with the DVD.

Added Note

TIP!

Remember the most important elements of a solo are not the notes but how you phrase them.

PLAYING WITH
D ROCK GROOVE

FROM
LET'S JAM! CD MORE BLUES & ROCK

Track 3 on the audio CD
included with this book.

1. Learn power chord shapes in D - p18

2. Play power chord shapes with the track - p18

3. Learn three licks with the track - p19

D ROCK GROOVE - RHYTHM

The rhythm for this track involves using only two fingers, the first and the pinky. Playing these two note power chords with a little bit of distortion creates a big sound.

31-32

Exercise 7

Pay attention to the pushes or the early chord changes in this pattern. For example, look closely at measure one and notice the chord change at the end of the measure. You will have to use your pinky to play much of this exercise. Practice this whole progression until it is easy to play, then try playing with the track.

Repeat 4 Times

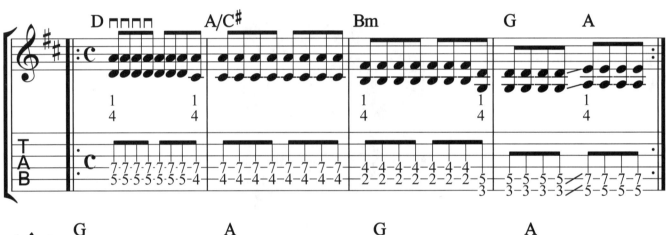

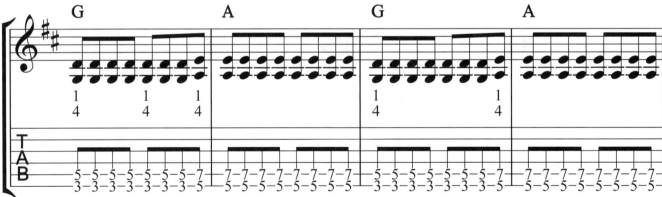

You can find the most common power chord shapes on pages 133-134 in *The Guitarist's Chord Book.*

TIP!

Practice scales slowly at first and then speed them up as you become more comfortable with them.

18

LICKS OVER D ROCK GROOVE

The three licks on this page are derived from the D major pentatonic scale.

DVD
VIDEO
34

Lick 7

This lick is all D major pentatonic. Practice it slow and smooth and then try it with the DVD.

DVD
VIDEO
35

Lick 8

This lick is a great example of D major extended pentatonic. Once you can play it easily, try it with the DVD.

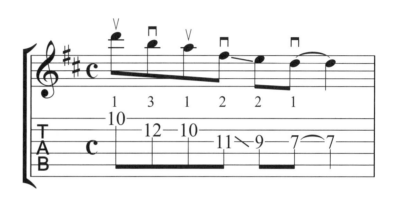

DVD
VIDEO
36

Lick 9

Watch the hammer ons in this lick. This lick sounds good all day long.

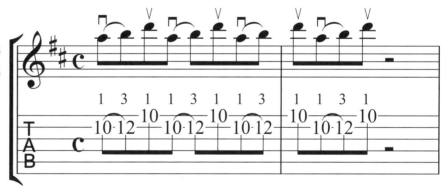

The five positions of the D major pentatonic scale can be found on page 46 of *The Guitarist's Scale Book*. These licks can be played any time over this particular track and sound good.

TIP!
Pay close attention to fingerings. The provided fingerings are designed to help you learn faster.

PLAYING WITH
Gm BLUES

FROM
LET'S JAM! CD MORE BLUES & ROCK

Track 4 on the audio CD
included with this book.

1. Learn Gm7, Cm7, & Bb13 arpeggios - p21

2. Play arpeggios along with the track - p22

3. Learn three licks and play with the track - p23

ARPEGGIOS OVER Gm BLUES

A good way to get familiar with a song and it's chord changes is to play a constant stream of arpeggios over the chords. An **arpeggio** is playing one note of a chord at a time.

Arpeggios over G minor

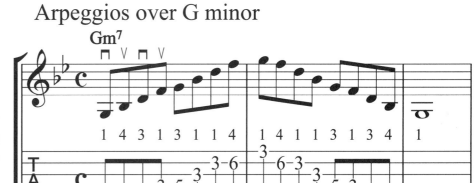

DVD VIDEO 38

Exercise 8

This is a two octave G minor arpeggio pattern. Practice it until it is smooth and easily played.

Arpeggios over C minor

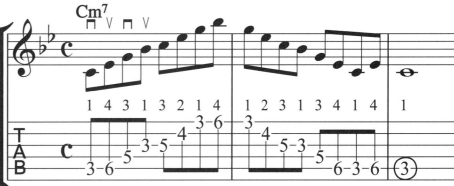

DVD VIDEO 39

Exercise 9

This is a two octave C minor arpeggio pattern. Watch the fingerings and practice it slowly.

Turnaround Arpeggios

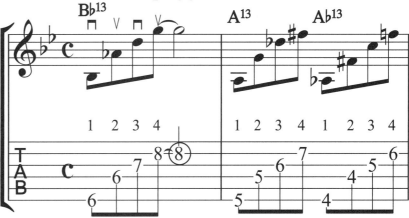

DVD VIDEO 40

Exercise 10

These are three different arpeggios played over the turn-around section of this track. It is the same shape, moving down one fret at a time.

Find more suggestions for arpeggio patterns starting on page 70 in the appendix of *The Guitarist's Lick Book*.

21

ARPEGGIOS COMBINED

This next exercise will combine all of the arpeggios we have learned into a long stream of notes played over the tune. When you finish, just start over again and play as many times with the track as you like.

G MINOR BLUES DRILL

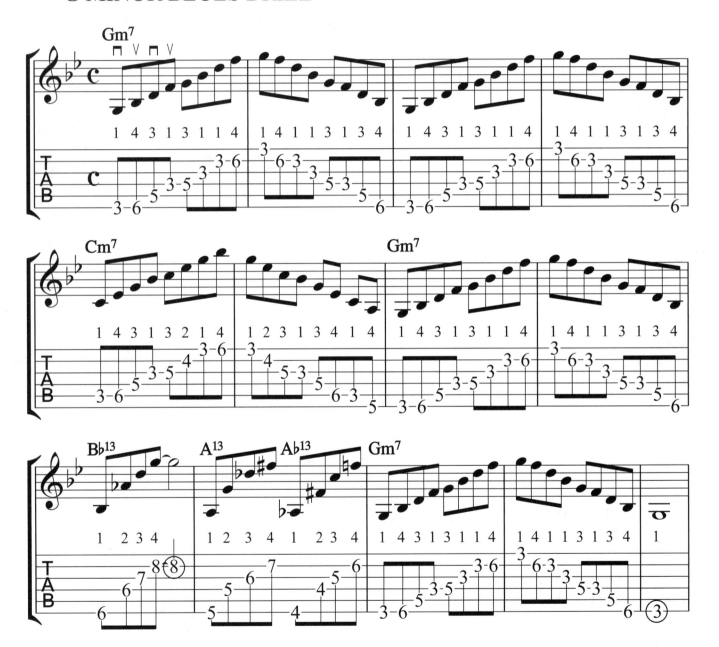

TIP!
A good guitar teacher can speed up your improvement by 200 to 300 percent.

22

LICKS OVER Gm BLUES

Here are three interesting licks out of the G minor pentatonic scale. The G natural minor scale could also be used.

 Lick 10

This lick starts with a bend. It comes out of the second position G minor pentatonic scale.

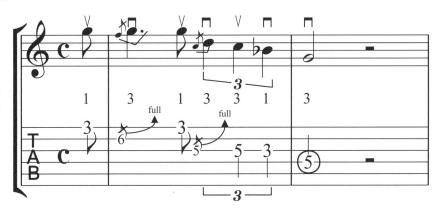

 Lick 11

This lick is out of the first position G minor pentatonic scale. Be careful with the rhythms.

 Lick 12

This lick has a stock bend and interesting rhythms. Remember, the more interesting the rhythms, the more interesting the player.

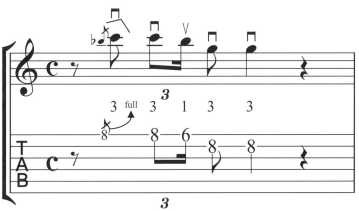

If you don't understand the difference between G minor pentatonic and the G natural minor scale, try reading *The Guitarist's Music Theory Book*. More licks in G minor can be found in Section 3 of *The Guitarist's Lick Book*.

PLAYING WITH
NOT TOO EXCITED

FROM
LET'S JAM! CD MORE BLUES & ROCK

1. Learn Cm7, Fm7, Abmaj7, and G7#9 - p25

2. Learn strum patterns to *Not Too Excited* - p26

3. Play *Not Too Excited* chord progression with track - p27

4. Learn three licks with the track - p28

STRUM PATTERNS FOR
NOT TOO EXCITED

Here is another chance to practice your rhythm playing. Try playing the chords and staying in time. Playing in time will be the most valuable technique you ever develop on guitar. ***Remember, guitar is a percussive instrument***.

 Exercise 11

Practice these chords.

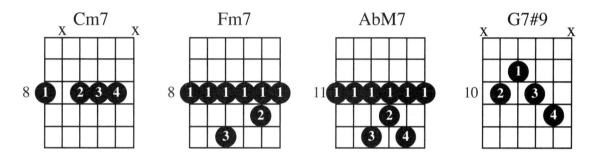

 Exercise 12

Practice changing chords with the track. In this exercise, we are not trying to play the rhythm pattern heard during the track. Only strum one time on the first beat of every measure until the last bar, when you strum one time on beat **two** of the measure.

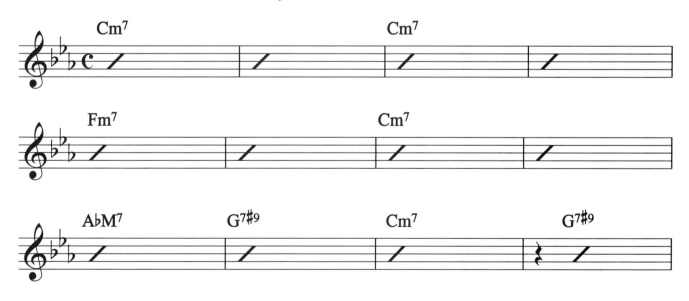

TIP!

Have strap locks installed on your guitar. It will help keep your guitar from falling.

Exercise 13

Practice this strum pattern while playing the C minor seven chord and the F minor seven chord.

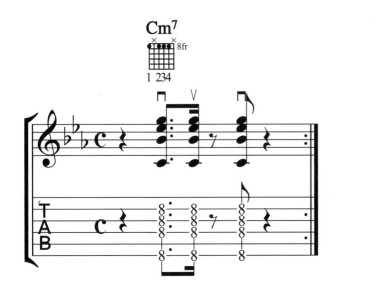

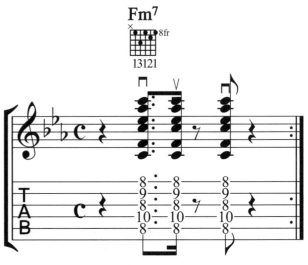

Exercise 14

Practice the strum pattern below while playing the A flat major seven chord and the G seven sharp nine chord.

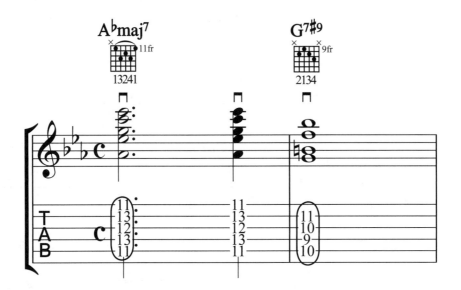

TIP!

If you're having trouble with rhythm, try a drum machine instead of a metronome. It can give you more subdivisions of the beat.

26

NOT TOO EXCITED - RHYTHM

Practice playing the strum pattern and the chord changes along with the DVD.

TIP!

*Put lemon oil on your fretboard every couple of months when
you're changing strings.*

LICKS OVER NOT TOO EXCITED

These licks are great C minor pentatonic licks. The second and third licks on this page actually use the C blues scale. This scale is often confused with the minor pentatonic scale because of it's similarity. The blues scale, however, has an added flat fifth.

Lick 13

This lick has a very bluesy sounding bend. Make sure the bend gets up a full step.

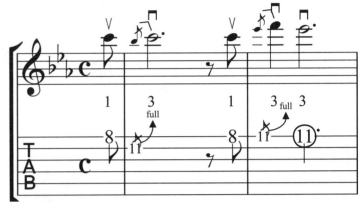

Lick 14

This lick involves pull offs and the blues note. Practice it slowly until you are comfortable with it and then try it with the DVD.

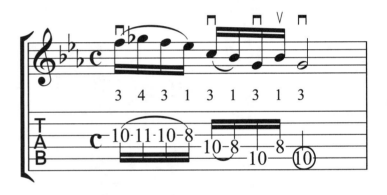

Lick 15

The lick starts with a **double stop,** which is simply two notes played at the same time. This lick also has a blues note.

More detailed theory explaining the blues scale can be found on page 41 inside *The Guitarist's Music Theory Book.*

TIP!
When finishing a gig, pack up your guitars first. It prevents damage.

28

MOVING A LICK AROUND OVER G SHUFFLE

FROM
LET'S JAM! CD BLUES & ROCK

1. Learn three licks - p30

2. Learn a solo to play with the track - p31

USING THE SAME LICK IN DIFFERENT PLACES

Over this track, learn to play the same lick at different places on the guitar so it works over each chord. Start by learning the lick over the G chord.

Lick 16

This lick is a major pentatonic lick in G. Practice it slowly at first.

Lick 17

This lick is a major pentatonic lick in C. It is the same as Lick 16 but higher up the neck.

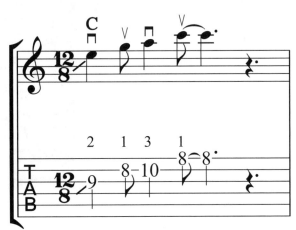

Lick 18

This lick is a major pentatonic lick in D. This is once again the same lick as Lick 16, but higher up the neck.

TIP!
Have your guitar set up twice a year and it will play easier and more in tune.

ALL THREE LICKS

This next exercise will give you a chance to practice this lick over the track and over each chord.

TIP!

*If you're going to stand when performing, you should
occasionally practice while standing.*

PLAYING WITH ROCK'N BLUES IN G

FROM
LET'S JAM! CD JAZZ & BLUES

1. Learn power chord shapes in G - p33

2. Learn to play strum patterns - p33

3. Play rhythm with the track - p34

4. Learn three licks with the track - p35

OLD SCHOOL ROCK RHYTHM WITH ROCK'N BLUES IN G

This track has Chuck Berry style rock rhythms. Practice this style of playing with the track. Start by learning the rhythm pattern.

Exercise 15

This is the rhythm to play over the G chord. These shapes are variations of power chords.

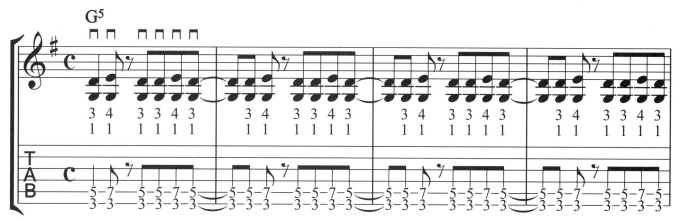

Exercise 16

This is the rhythm to play over the C chord. It is very similar to the rhythm we learned in the previous exercise. Just move it down to the 5th string.

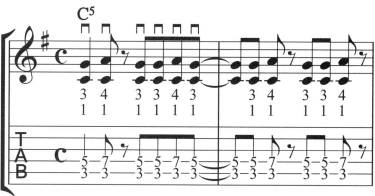

Exercise 17

This is the rhythm over the D chord. Once again, it is very similar to the previous two exercises. Practice all three of these licks with an emphasis on clarity so both notes are being heard.

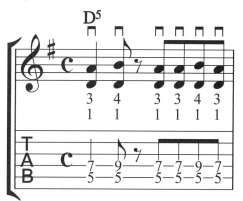

ROCK'N BLUES IN G - RHYTHM

Next we'll put all the chord changes together. Practice this slowly until it is smooth and then try playing along with the DVD.

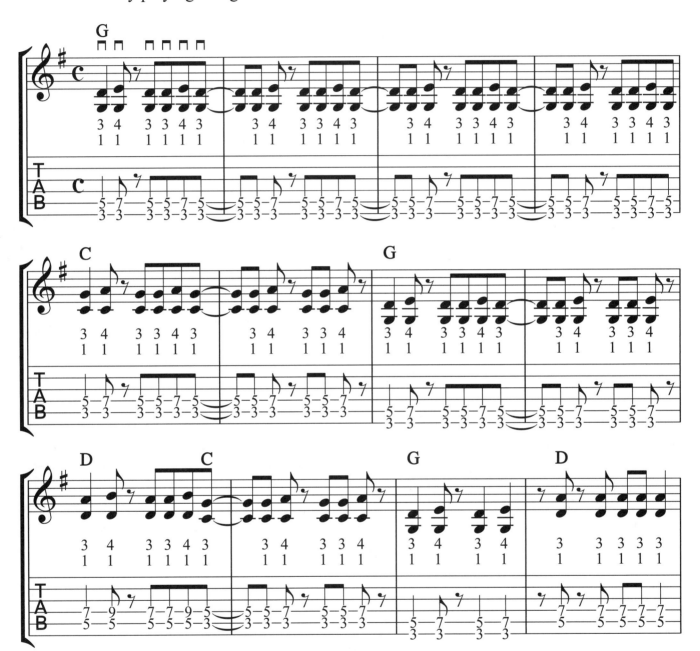

TIP!
*Standard effects used by guitar players include chorus,
distortion, digital delay, and wah pedals.*

34

LICKS OVER ROCK'N BLUES IN G

Practice these old school rock licks in G. Once you get them down, try playing with the track.

 Lick 19

This lick is an old school rock and roll lick. Make sure the bends get all the way up.

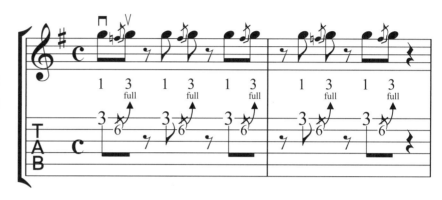

 Lick 20

This is another old rock and roll lick. Keep the double stops clear and the bend must reach a whole step.

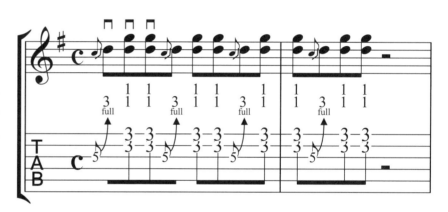

 Lick 21

This lick starts with a tiny quarter step bend. It doesn't quite reach the next fret. Practice it slowly and evenly until it is smooth.

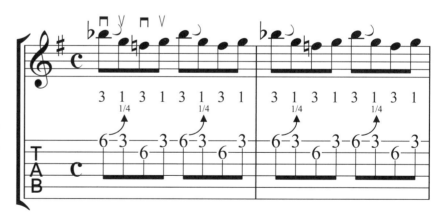

TIP!

If your tube amplifier is making noises, it may need new tubes.
Have it checked out.

PLAYING WITH FUNK IN E

FROM
LET'S JAM! CD BLUES & ROCK

1. Learn E9 and E13 chords - p37

2. Learn strum pattern for the track - p37

3. Play rhythm with the track - p37

2. Learn three licks with the track - p38

RHYTHM OVER FUNK IN E

We'll play a funky rhythm pattern over this track. There are no chord changes in this track, just variations of an E dominant chord. Practice the chord, the rhythm pattern, and then try it over the track.

Exercise 18
Practice the E9 chord and the E13 chord until you can make them relatively easily.

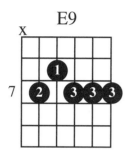
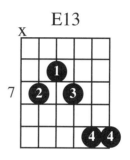

PLAY WITH THE TRACK

Now try combining the chord and the strum pattern over the track.

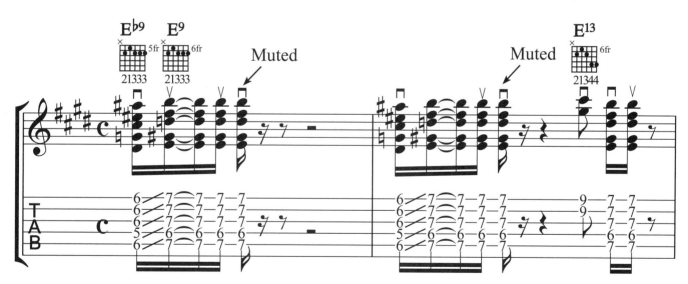

You can find more variations of the E dominant chord in *The Guitarist's Chord Book*. If you don't know what a dominant chord is, you should read *The Guitarist's Music Theory Book* (p70).

TIP!
When first starting to play, warm up slowly so you won't injure yourself.

LICKS OVER FUNK IN E

DVD VIDEO 76

The first two licks are out of the E major pentatonic scale. The third one is an old school octave bending lick.

DVD VIDEO 77

Lick 22

This lick comes out of the E major pentatonic scale and has many great chord tones in it. Practice slowly and smoothly and then try it over the track.

DVD VIDEO 78

Lick 23

This lick uses a hybrid minor and major pentatonic approach. Make sure the bend gets up a whole step.

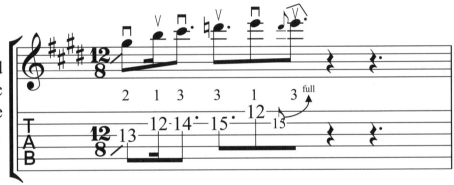

DVD VIDEO 79

Lick 24

This lick moves up the neck using a double stop. The double stop contains a whole step bend that must be accurate for the lick to sound right.

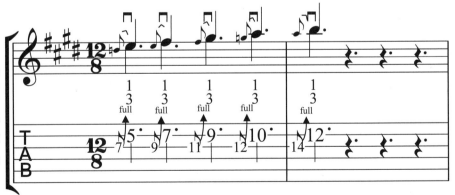

All five positions of the E major pentatonic scale can be found on page 48 of *The Guitarist's Scale Book*. Section 5 of *The Guitarist's Lick Book* has many more licks in E major.

TIP!
Take short breaks when practicing to allow your hands and arms to relax.

PLAYING WITH ROADHOUSE IN A

FROM
LET'S JAM! CD JAZZ & BLUES

1. One note at a time drill with the track - p40-41

2. Learn three licks with the track - p42

3. Learn a solo with the track - p43

ONE NOTE AT A TIME DRILL

This drill is great exercise for anyone learning to improvise or someone wanting to refresh their improvising skills. In this exercise, we will begin by picking one note out of a scale and using only that note against a track. We will then pick two notes and improvise using only those two notes. We then pick three and so on. This will cause us to focus on the important tools for improvising, the first being **rhythm**. We also have **dynamics** (loud and soft), **techniques** (slides, slurs, vibrato, etc), **tone** (brightness and softness of sound), and **phrasing** (an all-encompassing term meaning the combination of all of the above). Many players focus too much on the notes or pitches they are playing and not enough on the other more important elements of improvising. In this section, be sure to watch the DVD closely in order to get the most out of these exercises.

Exercise 19

Review the A minor pentatonic scale since this is the scale we will be using.

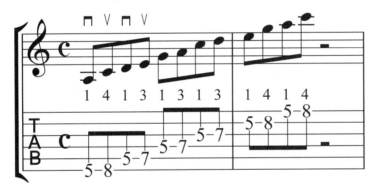

Exercise 20

Using only the note selected in this exercise, try to play something interesting. Listen to the audio example for help but do not imitate it. Use interesting rhythms and dynamics to make this exercise work.

TIP!
Never practice electric guitar barefoot in the basement.

Exercise 21

Using only the two notes selected in this exercise, try to play something interesting. Listen to the DVD for help. Use interesting rhythms, dynamics and techniques to make this exercise work.

Exercise 22

Using only the three notes selected in this exercise, try to play something interesting. Listen to the DVD for help. Use interesting rhythms, dynamics and techniques to make this exercise work.

Exercise 23

Using only the four notes selected in this exercise, try to play something interesting. Listen to the DVD for help. Use interesting rhythms, dynamics and techniques to make this exercise work.

After doing these exercises, gradually increase the number of notes until you are using all the notes in the scale. Take these ideas and expand your horizons using all the different positions of the scale you are using. No matter what notes you are using, remember to use rhythms, dynamics, techniques, tone and phrasing to make it interesting.

TIP!

Experiment with different styles of guitar playing. You never know where your next breakthrough moment will come from.

LICKS OVER ROADHOUSE IN A

These three licks are great sounding blues licks in A.

DVD
VIDEO
87

Lick 25

This lick starts with the A minor pentatonic scale and then throws in the major third of the A major scale.

DVD
VIDEO
88

Lick 26

This lick starts in A major pentatonic and then throws in the minor third for flavor. Watch the double stop and bend in the second measure.

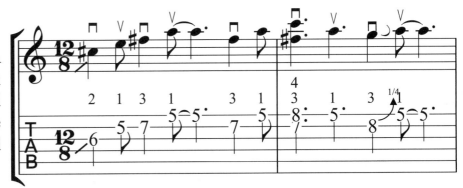

DVD
VIDEO
89

Lick 27

This lick is A minor pentatonic all the way.

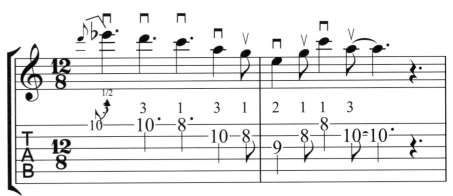

All the positions of the A minor pentatonic scale can be found on page 54 of *The Guitarist's Scale Book*. You can find the A major pentatonic scales on page 41 of the same book.

TIP!
Jam along CDs such as the Let's Jam! CD series are great ways to try out new licks and scales.

ROADHOUSE IN A SOLO

This solo is a combination of the previous three licks. Practice this solo first without the track at a reduced speed then play it with the track.

PLAYING WITH
E BLUESY ROCK

FROM
LET'S JAM! CD MORE BLUES & ROCK

1. Learn E, C#m7, A6/9, & B11 - p45

2. Learn strum pattern for the track - p45

3. Play rhythm with the track - p46

4. Learn three licks over the track - p47

5. Learn solo with the track - p48

RHYTHM OVER E BLUESY ROCK

This rhythm track is somewhat busy with a lot of strumming. You must also be able to move up and down the neck playing chords.

Exercise 24

First practice these chords.

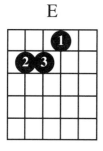
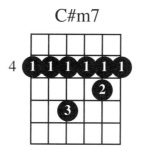
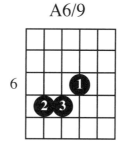
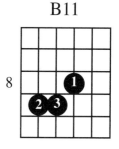

Exercise 25

Learn this strum pattern while playing the E major chord.

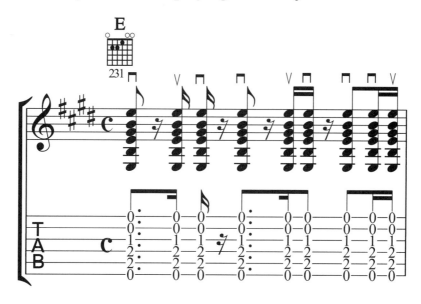

TIP!
*Use an electronic tuner to stay in good tune. They are
inexpensive and user friendly.*

CHORDS & STRUM PATTERN

Now try combining the chord changes and the strum pattern. Once you can play it smoothly, try playing along with the track.

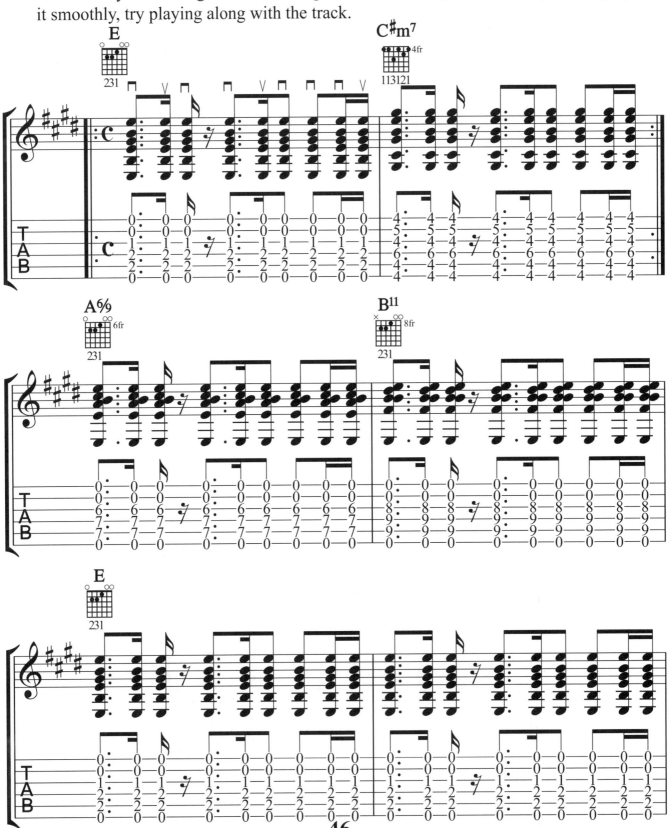

46

LICKS OVER E BLUESY ROCK

These three licks are E major licks. The first lick uses the E major diatonic scale. The second and third licks use the E major pentatonic scale.

Lick 28

This lick is an E major diatonic lick. Let the notes in the first measure ring together for a cascading effect.

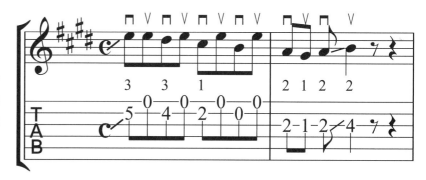

Lick 29

This is an E major pentatonic lick. Watch the fingerings so it plays smoothly.

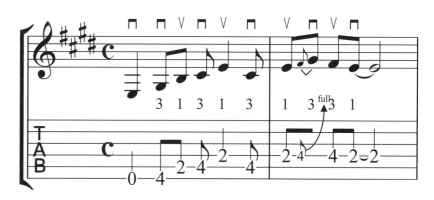

Lick 30

There are lots of hammer ons in this lick. You can repeat this lick all day and sound good.

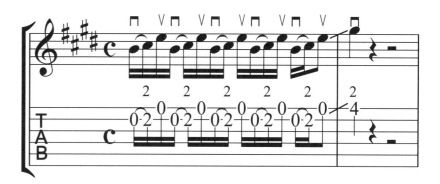

To understand what pentatonic and diatonic scales are, check out Section 3 of *The Guitarist's Music Theory Book*.

TIP!
Keep many extra picks around. They like to disappear, much like socks.

E BLUESY ROCK SOLO

This is our last solo. Remember solos are usually a combination of licks, scales, arpeggios, or other ideas. For this solo we have simply combined the last 3 licks and put them in an order that makes sense. Practice this solo first without the track and at a reduced speed. Once you are proficient, try it up to speed with the band on the DVD.

TIP!
Slow practice and relaxation are keys to becoming a better guitar player.

48

APPENDIX

CHORD CHARTS

You'll need the chord charts for the ten *Let's Jam! CD* tracks used in this course and included on the audio CD. The CD icon indicates the track number on the CD.

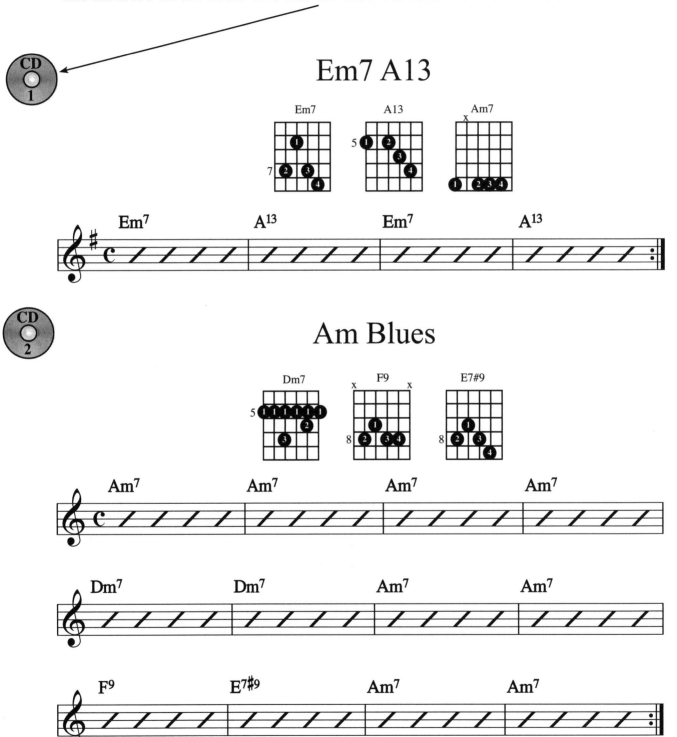

Em7 A13

Am Blues

D Rock Groove

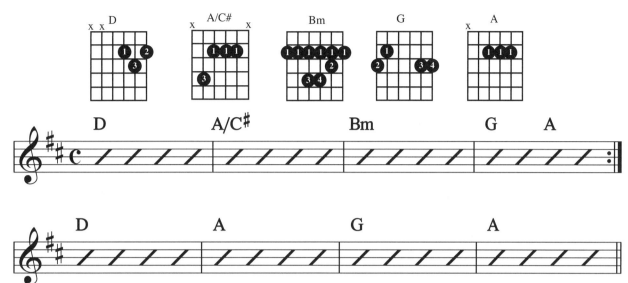

Gm Blues

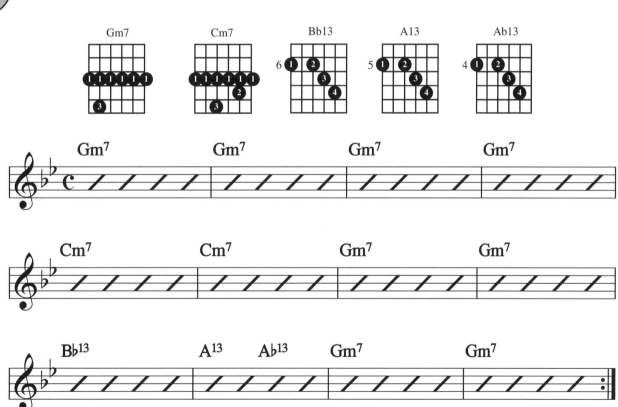

51

Not Too Excited

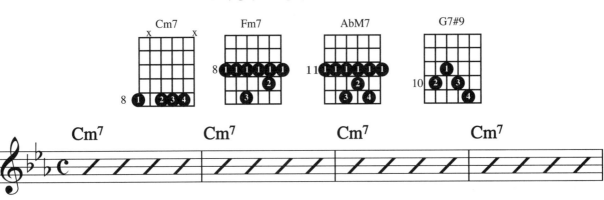

G Shuffle

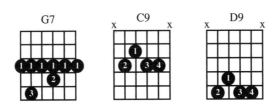

Rock'n Blues In G

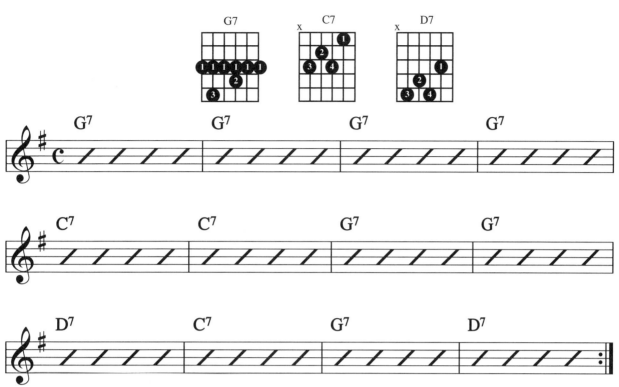

Funk In E

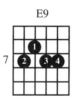

53

Roadhouse In A

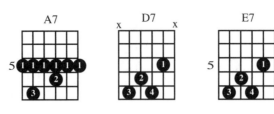

E Bluesy Rock

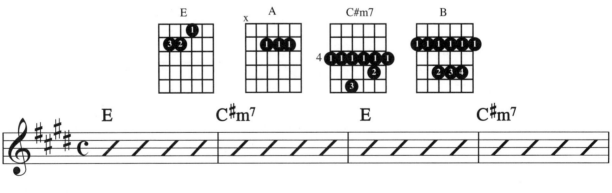

NOTES

WHERE TO GO NEXT

Taking private lessons from a qualified teacher is always a good idea. Check with your local music store to find a good instructor.

After completing this course, we have the *Guitarist's Jam System,* which includes six books and seven *Let's Jam! CDs*. This in an integrated learning course that will expand your playing ability, understanding of music, and help you learn to play with others. Check with your local music store or check out the website:

FreeGuitarVideos.com.

The Guitarist's Jam System

Tab	Chord	Scale	Theory	Note Reading	Lick

The Let's Jam! CD Series

Blues & Rock	More Blues & Rock	Blues & Rock Vol 3	Country & Bluegrass	Jazz & Blues	Hard Rock	Unplugged

These products are available at your local music store or send a check including $5.00 shipping and handling to:

Watch & Learn, Inc
1882 Queens Way
Atlanta, GA 30341
800-416-7088